FRATERNAL LIGHT

Wick Poetry First Book Series

Fraternal Light

On Painting While Black

Poems for Beauford Delaney

Poems by

A rlene Keizer

The Kent State University Press

Kent, Ohio

The Wick Poetry Series is sponsored by the Stan and Tom Wick Poetry Center and the Department of English at Kent State University.

Cataloging information for this title is available at the Library of Congress.

27 26 25 24 23   5 4 3 2 1

for my brother Brian and Chateau Noir,
in loving remembrance

For light, the queen of colours, pervades all that I see, wherever I am throughout the day, and by the ever-changing pattern of its rays it entices me even when I am occupied with something else and take no special note of it. It wins so firm a hold on me that, if I am suddenly deprived of it, I long to have it back, and if I am left for long without it, I grow dispirited.
—St. Augustine, Book X of *Confessions,* trans. R. S. Pine-Coffin

I left New York for Paris in 1953, and I have painted with greater freedom ever since. I tried to paint light, different kinds of light, and my painting has been associated with "abstraction." But there are no precise limits for me between "abstract" and "figurative" paintings . . .

I wish to be able to work one year free from immediate financial worries, in a quiet place, with the possibility of some travel in Europe.
—Beauford Delaney, application for funding

CONTENTS

FOREWORD

"One art calls out; another art answers."
—Preface to *Fraternal Light*

Arlene Keizer's rich and powerful new book on the art and life of African American painter Beauford Delaney, *Fraternal Light: On Painting While Black,* gives us much to consider; the art, the artist, the locations, the longings, the struggles, the journey of becoming. Most of all, I greatly admire how she handles light in these lines; regathered, translated anew, passionately relit in both the subjects and the readers' minds. Delaney's work and life story is in very good hands, and unlike his canvas, Keizer's poems give us not only the end result of an original eye and the stroke of a brush but the context and heat of the world and time that triggered it. We read and are arrested by the double beauty. Delaney's art calls; Arlene Keizer's poetry answers. We leave her book with eyes adjusted.

Cornelius Eady
Hodges Chair, the University of Tennessee–Knoxville
Cofounder, The Cave Canem Foundation

PREFACE

The great African American painter Beauford Delaney, born in Knoxville, Tennessee, in 1901, was a twentieth-century survivor. Raised in the segregated South by John Samuel Delaney, a Methodist Episcopal minister and barber, and Delia Delaney, whose artistry as a seamstress, quilter, gardener, and provider influenced him greatly, he began drawing, painting, and performing music in childhood. Beauford and his younger brother Joseph—who also became a renowned painter—remembered the economic privation of their domestic life being leavened by intense care, playfulness, religious devotion, and communal performances of sacred and secular songs. Of his parents' ten children, only Beauford and three brothers would live to adulthood.

Delaney was apprenticed to a white Knoxville painter while still in high school, and in 1923, he left Knoxville for Boston to get the rudiments of a formal education in drawing and painting. He privately acknowledged his love and sexual desire for men during his years in that city. In 1929, recognizing that he had absorbed and exhausted what Boston's cultural scene had to offer, Delaney moved to New York City.

Through a combination of artistic skill, consistent labor, and ingenuity, Delaney became a successful modernist painter, a fixture in the bohemian art scene in Greenwich Village in the 1930s, '40s, and early '50s. He was a companion and an inspirational figure to a multiethnic, international group of musicians, writers, and other visual artists, including Selma Burke, Cab Calloway, Don Freeman, W. C. Handy, Henry Miller, and Georgia O'Keeffe. Delaney met the young James Baldwin in 1940: an encounter that changed both their lives and about which much has been written. Eventually following Baldwin and other Black expatriates, Delaney migrated to Paris in 1953. The relative freedom from racial violence available to him in Europe at that time—as well as the particular light he found in Paris and the Mediterranean—facilitated his turn to abstraction and refinement of his signature style of expressionist portraiture. Finally overwhelmed by the mental health problems that had plagued him since late adolescence, he died in 1979 in a psychiatric hospital in Montparnasse, his beloved neighborhood.

Amazing Grace: A Life of Beauford Delaney, David Leeming's biography of the painter, records the presence of an unknown Black woman at Delaney's interment in the Montrouge Cemetery on the outskirts of Paris in 1979. "At the simple graveside service were a few of Beauford's closest friends—Charley Boggs, Jim and Bunny LeGros, Joseph [Delaney, his brother] and Ogust [Mae Delaney Stewart, his niece], and a mysterious young black woman whom no one recognized" (199). In *Fraternal Light*, I imagine the perspective of this figure. A scholar and poet, she excavates the public life of this extraordinary artist to illuminate private battles, losses, and triumphs—individual, familial, and communal. One art calls out; another art answers. This is a work of empathic speculation. It reaches out for emotional, intellectual, creative, and spiritual kinship, however fictive. Recognizing the paradigmatic nature of Delaney's struggle as a Black artist in the twentieth century, these poems offer a diasporic ceremony of remembrance, a meditation on the miracles of his survival, productivity, and longevity.

GROUNDING PRAYER: TO PAPA BOIS

Of course a god like you
must be queer—quixotic
and multiloving as you are—
      at home
            in so many bodies.

Desire's elliptical possibilities
define the forms you can take,
delineate your leaves, horns, hooves
      brown trunk
            black pelt
                      eyes
    changeable as vision.

    ###

What binds together
      obscure deity, sister witnessing,
          brotherhood of black gay men
          who met in Washington Square
        (immortal, middle-aged, deceased,
                      respectively)?
The need for
        feeling given form
the consecration
of new images arranged
in a future grammar.

The injunction:
        objectify this joy!

I. IN COUNTRY

TERROR IN THE HEART OF FREEDOM

1919   1969

Knoxville is green and gold and
black, with a red sun rising or
a blood moon falling.

                        Climate is to weather as
                        langue is to parole, as
                        color spectrum is to palette.

Your talent has no limits except
Vine Street/Knoxville/Tennessee/
Appalachia/the South . . .

                        The future arrived today: tongues
                        of fire no longer prophesy but burn
                        your literal house to the ground.

Sound and color—you make your home
out of what's immanent, knowing
already what you'll never own.

                        Always there's the presence that
                        watches, listens, smells, and judges.
                        Eyes, ears, nose, and ego

never wholly your own unless
liberated by wine, or moonshine.
Let's get real: what black man

                        born before '69 had a chance
                        at freedom unassisted by sloe gin
                        and reefer, the Invisible Man's

two-fisted high? Certainly not you,
terrified inside and out, your urges
reign in your body like whites rule

your lost hometown. Your father's god—
lord of mirth or mercy? Even now
you can't be sure where the laughter

comes from. How will you survive
the journey away from everyone who
loves you, and the predictable enemy?

How did you survive? How did you
weave a net to break your fall,
find freedom in the heart of terror?

SPRING IN BOSTON

This morning: the dew
on high grass and low,
on asphodel and

on all the unsung flowers.

QUARRY (AT THE ISABELLA STEWART GARDNER MUSEUM)

"His quarry was a suitable subject, his trophy the creation of a thing of beauty."

1. Worship

Sunday concerts at Fenway Court
sometimes take the place of services.
Once you pay the toll of discomfort
this music is free, like the filtered sunshine,
and the poor man's grand tour, courtesy
of Mrs. Gardner (whose panache,
while legendary, pales before
the lifesaving bravura in the angle
of an AME churchwoman's hat).

> Handel lifts you in your seat
> and sets your profile
> against a gold ground—
> the sunny side of the room,
> where light slants in from the atrium.
> Transubstantiation of chords
> into colors, stroking that place
> behind your eyes where
> tint and timbre meet.

How to rhythmize shades, conjure a stained glass effect
from the choral reality of their splendor? Fuse
the memory of hunger, the colored section, and the fiery chariot
of the Boyd Chapel choir? How to render
the dream that lets you hit that number?

In the seconds of silence before the applause,
you assume Sister's grace like
the mantle of Elijah.

You hold
yourself more carefully
as you leave the museum,
the vessel of your flesh
more precious now you're aware
of being molded by memory
and not yet fired.

Ω Ω Ω

"The knowing of the young male here is a constant comfort and also a menace."

2. I Wonder as I Wander (In the Monk's Garden)

Is it a coincidence that he's here again, third Sunday
in a row? Is he looking at me? Does he
work here or live nearby? Are these his
hunting grounds? Is he playing with
my gaze or stalking desire? Just out
for a walk and a smoke? What would his hand,
his fist,   deliver?

Ω Ω Ω

"I think of this garden as the sunken garden of Western civilization."

3. Outdoor Interior

A dead god beckons
          you into the courtyard,
bobs his falcon head to acknowledge
          the only other African
under this depleted sun.
          You borrow his eyes
for the next stage of your journey.

BLUE HARLEM

New York, 1929

(from) Boston (all alone) money

Harlem street 130th Street rooming houses

sign window "room for rent" bell woman

bell room (two) weeks baggage rent

(2) hours time number house work

room number bell woman door (chilly) voice

room man name Bob guy (out for) trouble

room life man terms nothing belongings

(alone) night night New York City bus

Village

14th Street Union Square (west) cigarette (the)

depression people people work food place sleep

(a) stranger nothing dollars pocket soul mind idea

difference masses people nothing

camaraderie understanding chance

multitude people races night lives

parks cafes mood kind stimulation

fancies something: force will courage

terror? fear? city everything calm determination

determination the young state shock

cups coffee rolls things

(myself)

natives New York City millions day

challenge (it)

FOUND METAPHOR

a queen of spades
      facedown on the pavement
her cheeks   her palms pockmarked
     by gravel

        in this neighborhood
the voice of the law—
      truncheon swing, siren, bullhorn soundwave—
           travels on every breeze

even a joker knows
     when to assume
         the position

SISTER

diminished
          dwindled.

She was supposed to live
for you

          but dwindled
because of
      /   despite

the provisions
      and
          the need.

Ragtime's fine struts still hold up
the edifice of jazz: the left hand's
drum or walking bass line, the right's
        breakaway terpsichore and return,
        temporary 5/4 time and the luck
        to be black on a Saturday night.

Pain and joy are born together
like Esau and clever Jacob,
but hunger won't convince you
to barter your birthright.

        A boy climbs the stairs to your door.
        When you open it, his eyes reflect
        a melancholy glow from
        the jury-rigged overhead light.

The Victrola heats up one side
of your room, while the potbellied stove
        barely warms the other. Ice blocks
        get chipped up in the bathtub for
        rum punch and G-and-Ts. No greater love
for one another than the rent party,
impromptu jam or fête celebrating
a one-man show. 181 Greene Street
        is cradle, eyrie, gallery,
        birdcage, and tiny nightclub playing
"The Easy Winners" for cakewalk moves
that years ago shed the plantation's
enervated soil.

                By now,
you're painting syncopation,
the deep cadence of black life: two
        steps forward and a calculated
half-step back, a flyweight's footwork,
the heart's stutter step when we know
        we've found someone to love   again.

DARK RAPTURE 1941

The tropical forest travels
with Papa Bois, with
his power, is
the force of flowering.

Oh, what we can do   when the right gods
watch over us.

The garret studio vanishes
under a visual fantasia—
cool light   the full spectrum—
red orange yellow green blue indigo violet.
At the center is green
heightened by black, lightened
by white.   Two trees
announce that the body
and the throne and the wood
are one.

Oh, what we can do   when the eyes of love
are upon us.

The subject of the dream is
the dreamer. The landscape
sings the painter's wish fulfillment—
improvised pastoral symphony,
syncopated rite of spring.

Our music has never failed us,   never
failed us.

GRATITUDE

I realize I cannot fulfill it, lord,
but thank you   for this desire
that rises up with me each morning
and goes to bed with me
each blessèd night.

HAZING THE AMIABLE BEAUFORD DELANEY

The Black Angel of Henry Miller

"Here I sit in Greene Street, said the canvases, and
I am invisible to all but
the eye of God. I am
the spirit of hunger for all that has been denied me,
one with the street,
one with the cold, dead walls.

But I am not dead, neither am I cold, nor
yet invisible. I am of darkest Africa a luminary,
an aurora borealis, a son of a slave
in whose veins courses the proudest
white blood. I sit here in Greene
Street and I paint what I am, my
mysterious mixed bloods, my inscrutable
mixed hungers, my elegant and most
aristocratic solitudes, my labyrinthine
prenatal remembrances. Here there are
no sun, moon or stars, no warmth, no
light, no companionship. But in me, *the*
amazing and invariable Beauford DeLaney,
are
    all the lights,
            all the stars,
                        all the constellations,
all the angels for companions.
                        I am
Greene Street as it looks from the angle of
eternity; I am a crazy nigger as he looks
when the Angel Gabriel blows his horn;
I am
        solitude playing

the xylophone to make
                the rent . . ."

SHADE

a rejoinder to "The Amazing and Invariable Beauford DeLaney"

█████████ in Greene Street ████████████
██████ invisible to all but
the eye of God█
the spirit of hunger████████████████
one with the street

████████████████████

███████ not dead██████████cold███
█ invisible ███ of dark ██████ a luminary,
an aurora borealis, a son of a slave
███████████████ proud ███
██████blood. I sit here in Greene
Street and I paint ████████ my
mysterious mixed bloods, my inscrutable
mixed hungers, my elegant and most
aristocratic solitudes, my labyrinthine
███████ remembrances. Here there are
no sun, moon or stars, no warmth, no
light, no companionship but █████ *the*
amazing and invariable Beauford DeLaney

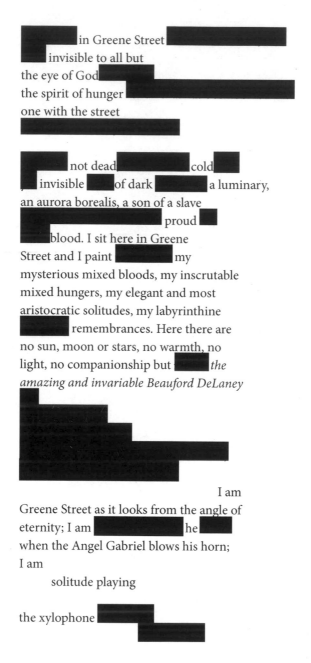

I am
Greene Street as it looks from the angle of
eternity; I am ██████████ he ████
when the Angel Gabriel blows his horn;
I am
solitude playing

the xylophone ████████████
████████████

INTERLUDE

I'm an eavesdropper and a voyeuse.

I like the smell of other people's

cooking, drifting up through the floorboards.

If I could taste and touch

vicariously,

      I would.

LEAVING GREENE STREET: BEAUFORD'S PSALM

You have raised me up
to the third floor
above the hustlers and rent boys
who taught me how to live
here.
       New punks beat me up
to claim their territory from
a "nigger queer," but I got
a few licks in: you have not
suffered my enemies
to rejoice over me.

I'm sailing for the City of Light
      of my own free will,
so that my glory may sing
      praise to you   and not be silenced.

II. ELSEWHERE

IN THE MUSÉE DE CLUNY

The Lady and the Unicorn

Naturally the monkey embodies desire—
teak hands hold up a Venetian red
berry of temptation. He smells
and tastes, a dumb show
of the way these senses lead to sin.

How did he get here, refugee from forgotten
Silk Road trades that made his pigment
possible? Now he can't be freed.

      You have to go further back
         in time, further down
            to the cold Roman level,
               the foundations laid when an African

could rise through the martial ranks
      in Lutetia or Londinium (before
         Shakespeare told that tale anew)
            to find another purpose
               for the brown homunculus

an older allegory.

               All that's gathered here
bows down to the white virgin
mother to-be enshrined
by new empires.

            You wander, enchanted,
mind saturated—finally—hurry
home with your last impression:
      a broken column holding aloft
      the head of the Queen of Sheba.

UNE BOÎTE DE NUIT

You meet him there
                              (speak easy)
full of terror and intent.

You'll disappear under the floor
if the cops come.
                              Pleasure
shivers your flesh
     before he touches you—
your canvas of need
                              his impasto—

Too much some will say
                              (quietly)
about your French abstractions
too much paint
                              (costly)
covering what was stretched
and bare.

His fingers rake your body
     raw umber, burnt sienna
delivering you into
     une nuit blanche:
the first of many
     sleepless Paris nights.

portrait of a man
portrait of a man in green
portrait of a man in sunlight
portrait of a man in red
portrait of a man in black

the fall

portrait of a man with petal background
portrait of a man in soft light
man in African dress

self-portrait in a Paris bath house

GOOD NEWS WILL COME TO YOU BY MAIL

Sister's Dreamnote from Knoxville

Mama's been telling the girls
to leave out any bad news,
just like you thought. They
don't want to burden you,
and they know you're keeping
the same ~~country-bred~~ silence.
                    ~~loving~~
          migrant

CANOPY

Like a tree, he interprets light.
Papa Bois, old woodsman, come see
how this golden son paints your domain—
sycamore's plainsong, pine's keen sigh,
aspen's conspiring laughter—be
a witness to his legerdemain.

> When branches thrash outside your window
> you sometimes believe you're the storm
> that moves them, displaced hurricane.
> You tell no one. That's nothing new.
> The South taught you early to conform,
> to wear a mask that's become urbane.

From star to star the mental optics rove.
If only your hard labor conjured love.

A COUNTRY METER

"Solvitur ambulando."/"It is solved by walking."

Tramping away from Paris
into the countryside, you're seen
as poor and odd, but
not as prey. You're too rare here
to be a threat. No one
offers you a ride either.

Free to stroll and stride and commit
colors to memory, free
to unpack easel and paint box
in a fallow field, at liberty
to set the sun
in its rightful place.

> *swing low, golden eagle,*
> *golden double, coming for to carry me*
> *up in the middle of the air*
> *steal away   steal away   o pray*
> *my wings are gonna fit me well*
> *I ain't got long to stay here*

Tramping this straight Roman road—
slave-built imperial trace—
you find that the voices
can't outsing you
when you're backed by
a chorus of fraternal light.

MANDALA

Untitled, c. 1958

Your vision will not be erased
    like colored sand.
The world glimpsed through
    your finished canvas
appears and disappears depending
    on our fluency
in its fractal language,
    our ability to follow
the movements of your hearing eyes,
    your seeking hands.

DRINK

a little libation:

        wet the heads

of the ancestors

        so you hear

"greyboy"

        and

        "auntie man"

as whispers

        not shouts

HOW CAN WE LIVE UNMAGNIFIED AMONG THE WHITE COLOSSI?

The Roads to Rhodes, 1961

On the train to Brindisi
    you imagine tracing the lean calf
        and cocked heel of the coastline.

Erotic dreams and the promise of Greek
    statues to sketch should throw
        the hellhounds off your trail, but

they navigate by the scent of fear
    and desire for the unknown, the essence
        of travel, in your experience.

I'm in the mood for an ode
    but all that comes is elegy
        mournful   documentary

following your oceanic journeys
    to a lost source, a monument
        kept alive by ancient gossip

which we all know is its own form
    of divinity. Rigorous faiths
        warn against depicting gods

as giant versions of men, but
    homo faber persists in making
        them in our own images.

I can't paint, but I've composed
    the perfect deity for you, when
        he can no longer help or harm you.

Why do I keep imagining
   you before his altar, in a grove
      of flame trees? *Abstraction #12*—

icon of the shapeshifting black source
   of our radiance. Accepting the first
      joyful mystery—your gifted hands—

you've drawn our intercessors who
   keep us believing black life is
      possible: Saint Phillis, Saint

Frederick, and holy Harriet
   wading in the water, children,
      birthing us from the womb of grief.

I have a magpie relationship to art—
   gold and gilt, silver and tin, emerald
      and leaf stems on a greenhouse floor—

satisfied by your blending of yellow
   with hallowed ochre (*Moving Sunlight*)
      and black men warming themselves around

can fires, pianos, and saxophones.
   Why does romantic love obsess you?
      Will questioning your yearning

save me from my own? Your muse is
   a beloved who loves you as a friend.
      His care will sustain you until the end.

What you seek is seeking you: one
   poet's promise and threat. You never
      made it to Rhodes, site of phantom

Helios, cut off at the knees
  before common era. The Ionian Sea—
    a siren song of blessèd silence.

Pleasure ties us to the mast of this life.
  A fisherman pulls you from the water.
    Joy blocks our ears or ties us

to the mast of this life. Amazing grace:
  rough kindness of strangers whose hands don't
    want you to die in their harbor.

QUESTIONNAIRE

a cinquain

pulsing
and quivering
what does your pain feel like,
on a scale of one to five where
one is

mild and
four horrible
five excruciating?
how does your pain change over time?
stabbing

boring
PUNCTATE PRESSURE
what does your pain feel like?
write the most appropriate word—
tender

THERMAL
which words describe
your pain at its worst?   hot
scalding TEMPORAL throbbing sharp
beating

spreading
how does your pain
change with time? how strong is
your pain?   nagging   nauseating
transient

which word
lacerating
describes your pain right now?

INCISIVE PRESSURE severing
smarting

more points
on an exam
you'd rather fail or skip
out on altogether   piercing
BRIGHTNESS

rhythmic
periodic
continuous: which word
describes the pattern of your pain?

steady

BLACK CANVAS

you would love this: a bole ready-made
for melancholy works, those paintings,
like your life, built up from dark to light

the savings on paint alone would buy you
a few more dinners with friends, a few more
tubes of transparent gold and Naples yellow

you might have used this black ground for night
visions through high windows in Clamart
and your rose madder portrait of Dante

    when you painted *Greece*
—nothing but harbor, edge to edge—
those blues would have rested upon
      an ocean bottom
as matte and gritty as anthracite

SISTER'S SPIRIT SHOUTS

Beauf, I saw your grown-man face in the water!

Beauf?

I just saw your grown-man face:
    a flash in the water
        eyes open, mouth sealed shut.

        Beauf?

I saw you grown, your own man face
    unpeaceful.
        Where in the water? I'd know you anywhere . . .

        Beauf?

Beloved boy, I caught a glimpse of you grown
    sown
        in the water.

MARIAN, ILLUMINATED

I.
Your portrait of her is a gilded mirror,
exactly your height, so you stand
eye to eye with your true likeness,
absent the shadows that follow light.

II.
What you have in common exceeds
the obvious. You both love Schubert—
"Ave Maria," "Death and the Maiden,"
"The Crucifixion"—he was prodigal.
He would have been right at home
in the black church; he knew
how many keep coming back for
the music alone.
                    Word of his death
reached Schubert early and he
sounded his own passing bells.
That's a black thing, if I ever
heard one. Genius, syphilitic.

III.
In her role model memoir,
Anderson laments the dearth of
gorgeous music in English for her voice.
She's signifying, gently, in the style
of the Philadelphia Negro.
Vienna crowned and sent her back
to Carnegie Hall a queen, but black
folks didn't need Toscanini
to tell us her contralto was
a voice heard once in a century.

IV.
Intimations of productive exile,
seeds first planted by your friend Countee

who knew that crossing the Atlantic
could cause black arts to multiply
like loaves and fishes. You planned

this painting for two decades,
since you and Jimmy met her backstage
after a New York show, so long ago
that her copper-and-tan skin is now
rendered with an orange so new you
couldn't afford it in the '40s.

V.
Order composed of mass, line, plane,
and color—a chromatic scale
where your beloved yellow falls,
vibrating, between *fa* and *sol*.
You both sing in the lowest register.

VI.
What is that thicket under
her left elbow? You've signed
your name on her right side,
refusing to block our view of that
bolus or briar patch, tangle of lost and
found edges representing—*at last*—
the obscurity of extreme precision.

PAPA BOIS DANS LA RUE VERCINGÉTORIX (1971)

"Green people are hope without reason."

When Papa Bois wanted to remind an aging painter
of the lushness of brown skin tones
   he wore a grass-green jacket
   and chartreuse pants
   tapered at the ankle,
   loosely knotted a cravat
   the color of a lacewing
   around his throat.
   He arranged himself in a maroon
   folding chair, applied lipstick
   in a truer red, and settled
   down to wait.

In your dream, the sky turned
the hue that heralds a tornado:
darkening absinthe.
                       You arose
with that spring afterimage,
layered it on canvas, baptizing
the muddy, drunken forehead of your world
with a chrism of light.

Portrait of a Young Musician:
   sunflower-yellow dreamwork holding
   the intricate, fitted mask
   of another's face.

JEAN GENET IN THE JUNGLE

this jingle is for Jean Genet in the jungle
a jungle jingle for Jean who joined les nègres
in the farcical colonial jungle:

voleur menteur mentor   writer of memoir
dedicated damné living a louche life   writing a wily
worlded life   masking masochism   Morocco-bound
Jean généreux   germinating in the jungle

FEBRUARY IN PARIS

overnight, the curtains froze
   in front of the cracked window

but in the courtyard the jays
   make a racket of spring

betting against the groundhog

NIGHT IN A CITY HOSPITAL

I fly down the corridors

    of the psych ward, hovering

        around the eye of the nurse's station,

past the phone booth—auditor of cries

        outside visiting hours—

    into the doorless rooms and over

the drugged and restlessly sleeping.

Cellophane wings barely keep me aloft,

    meaty angel, would-be guardian

        of dysphoric dreamers, especially

you, beloved brother, torchbearer.

    Is it true every creature on earth

        is witnessed from a higher plane?

Condescending love and pity

    poorly mask our envy: we

know your paintings are empirical

        evidence of things not seen.

COMING TO SAINT PAUL

An unsent letter to James Baldwin

53 rue Vercingétorix
Paris February 1972

Dearest Jimmy,

Your angels passed by my whatnot yesterday and gave me affection
and a longing to see you, to have the sweetness of your dear ones and
of course yourself. Have been working continuously on all sorts of
work and whatnot here in Paris. Let everyone lead the life that his
talent has assigned him, and to which art has called him. Yesterday
après midi I so wanted to arrive in your marvelous home in Saint Paul.
I have an inkling of coming down even if it is brief. Have been working
like a slave (smile) not really like a slave; am I not free? It's only
wanting to see our dear Jimmy and his dear family there in Saint Paul
that makes the work feel like drudgery. I bless you for the sweetness of
your dear babies who came emoting and full of gayety and pleasure.
I may come along to be with you—briefly—because there is so much
to do; however, it will give me great pleasure to see you (briefly) also.
I know you are always working and have very little time for visitors.
Also my need to see you is such a necessity (why am I in peril every
hour?) that I can come and stay 3 or 4 days and will come back full of
the splendor of you and your dear ones. I so enjoy the uniqueness of
Saint Paul; he is really "there."

My love to all of you, and if you are not moving from St Paul I will
drop by for 2 or 3 days to see you and your remarkable genius and
love. There is one glory of the sun, and another of the moon, and
another glory of the stars; for star differs from star in glory. God bless
all of you and I will come down to the glorious St Paul. I will visit you
after passing through Velizy, for I intend to pass through Velizy, and
perhaps I will stay with you or even spend the summer, so that you can
speed me on my journey, wherever I go. For I don't want to see you
now just in passing; I hope to spend some time with you, if the Lord
permits.

Be watchful, stand firm in your commitment to your art, be courageous, be strong. Let all that you do be done in love. God bless all of you!

Love, Beauford

WRITING YOU FROM A PLAGUE YEAR

"Is this why we sing through/these death marches?"

I was already thinking of you
before the dying began in earnest,
before hubris and hate delivered
ten thousand hecatombs of corpses.

    You knew all these losses:
    motherloss and brotherloss and
    fatherloss and piercing sisterloss,
       lived through pandemic and white riot,
    knew the fall of the self through
    immeasurable space and knew
    the feeling of the bottom coming up
    hard, under your hands and knees.

Did you ever wish for a less keen
eye, or corrective vision?
Teach me how to see clearly
to the final other side.

    Your sight is a four-stringed instrument
    tuned differently for every ceremony—
    sometimes a banjo
       whose gut strings stretch from Senegambia
    to the Carolinas,
    then a subtle cuatro, then
      a Mahalo ukulele,
    now a lute, now a lyre
    silent   in the rust-red hands of Orpheus.

MY MEMORY STAMMERS: BUT MY SOUL IS A WITNESS

Joe Delaney Remembers

Beauford was the chosen one
when we were kids.

> In New York,
> I watched a second self
> grow up beside him, lionized
> and patronized and sometimes so
> confused he really thought he might
> be Jesus.

Christ, I miss my brother's voice,
his hands and
> the family feeling.

FINAL PRAYER: TO BEAUFORD D. (1976)

In St. Anne's Hospital

You now wear the mature aspect
of the god himself:
  the fat maintained by human hungers
  burned away in the fire of your becoming
  Other—lean, inscrutable,
  surprisingly strong,
  a corona of white hair cradling
  your oaken face.

Eros eluded you.
                    Philos
kept you in the world
longer than any actuarial table
could have predicted
based on birthplace, race,
lifestyle, sustained exposure
to violence and acetone.

Destinations are one's true
  originations: from Byoo•ford
  to *Beau•fort!*
                    Philos
  kept you alive until
  you could permanently claim
  the high, holy silence
  of the light you sought.

A RITE

those of us who claim you as our ancestor
—our progenitor—
carve or forge or otherwise fashion
figurines with hollow bellies
we fill with okra seeds coins hog's hair
red Tennessee clay and graveyard dirt
from the cemetery at Thiais

we carry these graven images
into the forests that remain to us:
Jardin de Luxembourg   Central Park
the carefully tended woods in Saratoga Springs
Knoxville's old hickories
and the Boston Public Garden where
you copped your first feel and began
wrestling with angels in disguise

when darkness falls we place our new minkisi
among the trees   we sing
the songs that call down starlight

our icons are left alone with the night
awaiting your descent

ACKNOWLEDGMENTS

I was lucky to be born into a family that counts writing among the noble occupations. I'm deeply grateful for being imbued with a love of literature and art from my earliest days and for being allowed to indulge in reading and writing as spaces and practices of freedom. I carry my family with me always; they will find my love for them hidden in these pages. Dear Bri: I still can't believe you're gone.

I thank the friends, writers, scholars, and artists who saw me and offered me the kinds of encouragement and assistance one maker can lend another: Jim Richardson, Gwendolyn Brooks, Denise Levertov, Barbara Christian, Alfred Arteaga, Yusef Komunyakaa, Lorna Goodison, Marianetta Porter, Ngũgĩ wa Thiong'o, Amy Gerstler, Valentina Vavasis, Shawan Worsley, Laura Kang, Harryette Mullen, Titus Kaphar, Andy Young, Mireia Estrada of Jiwar, Casey Ruble, Wendel White, Catherine Sameh, Rosanna Bruno, Shayla Lawz, Andrea Stone, and James Hannaham.

I'm very grateful that the Michael Rosenfeld Gallery, acting on behalf of the Estate of Beauford Delaney, has allowed me to include Delaney's image, brief quotations from his journals, and an extended quotation from one of his unpublished letters. I've been reading Cornelius Eady's poetry since the 1980s, when I liberated *Victims of the Latest Dance Craze* from a private library. I feel incredibly honored by his choice of my manuscript.

The artist Nell Painter, also known as the renowned historian Nell Irvin Painter, gave permission for her Delaney-inspired drawings to appear on the covers of *Fraternal Light*. Thank you! I'm amazed and delighted that this book is being held in such hands as it makes its way into the world.

Roy Freeman responded with alacrity and joy (and drawings and photos) when I requested permission to include his father Don Freeman's tender sketch of Delaney reading a letter. I think of this drawing as an homage to Delaney's epistolary practices of survival.

Fraternal Light is informed, first and foremost, by James Baldwin's written and spoken testimonies about Beauford Delaney and by David Leeming's luminous biographies—*Amazing Grace: A Life of Beauford Delaney* and *James Baldwin: A Biography*. The quotations from Delaney's journals appearing in the poems were previously published in *Amazing Grace*. At the Beinecke Rare Book and Manuscript Library at

Yale University, where I held the Ruth Stephan Fellowship in fall 2022, my research was enriched by access to the David Leeming Collection of James Baldwin Research; Beauford Delaney Letters to Larry Wallrich; Beauford Delaney Letters to Don, Lydia, and Roy Freeman; and Portraits of Beauford Delaney (by Don Freeman), all in the James Weldon Johnson Collection in the Yale Collection of American Literature. I also consulted the Irene and William R. Rose Papers in the Yale Collection of American Literature. Special thanks to the Beinecke for providing a high-quality reproduction of Don Freeman's drawing of Beauford Delaney.

Research for this book was also funded by the Mellon Foundation and the Schomburg Center for Research in Black Culture's Scholars-in-Residence Program in 2021–22. I spent many hours reading Delaney's mail in the peerless Schomburg Center in Harlem; the support and fellowship of Marina Bilbija, Abosede George, Nina Angela Mercer, Stéphane Robolin, and Mercy Romero made those hours especially sweet. I thank the Schomburg curators and librarians, Tammi Lawson and Rhonda Evans in particular, for their knowledge and patience.

The archivist Shana McKenna at the Isabella Stewart Gardner Museum provided me with critical information about the Museum in the years Delaney frequented it. I thank the Archives of American Art at the Smithsonian for providing access to an audio interview between Joan French Seeman (-Robinson) and Beauford Delaney, the only recording of his voice that I was able to locate.

I drafted a significant portion of this book while supported by a residency: the Sketch Model Creative-in-Reference program at Olin College of Engineering, funded by a grant from the Mellon Foundation. I thank the Sketch Model team and Mellon for the critical gift of salaried time for creative pursuits during the 2020–21 academic year.

I also extend my thanks to the artists, curators, gallerists, art historians, and cultural critics who have worked to bring new attention to Delaney's magnificent oeuvre. Special recognition is due to the indefatigable Monique Y. Wells, who created and maintains the blog *Les Amis de Beauford Delaney*.

My extraordinary good fortune in winning the 2022 Stan and Tom Wick Poetry Prize has been extended through the kind handling of *Fraternal Light* by David Hassler, editor of the Wick Poetry Series and director of the Wick Poetry Center at Kent State, and the Kent State University Press, especially Mary Young and Susan Wadsworth-Booth.

I'm deeply grateful to Sharon Dolin and Marlon Ross for ushering my book into the world with their gracious, precise, and sizzling language. Thank you! For many years, your work has brought me joy, knowledge, and inspiration.

"Canopy" was published in *Poem-a-Day* by the Academy of American Poets on February 7, 2023. "Writing You from a Plague Year" will appear in *Obsidian: Literature and Arts in the African Diaspora,* Issue 49.1.

NOTES

Epigraphs:
Confessions, St. Augustine, trans. R. S. Pine-Coffin, Penguin, 1961/1984.

Beauford Delaney: Beauford Delaney Collection, Sc MG 59, Schomburg Center for Research in Black Culture. This excerpt from an application for fellowship funding and all other quotations from Delaney's letters, journals, and unpublished papers are reprinted by permission of the Michael Rosenfeld Gallery, on behalf of the Estate of Beauford Delaney.

"Grounding Prayer: To Papa Bois": Papa Bois is a Caribbean mythological figure; he presides over these poems. He is an embodiment and guardian of the forest and can take human form, especially that of a muscular, vital old man with horns and hooves (often hidden). I've interpreted his myth freely for the purposes of this collection. I imagine that Delaney came to Papa Bois's attention through the painter's deep friendship with Connie Williams, the Trinidadian owner of the Calypso Café on MacDougal Street, one of Delaney's regular haunts in the Village. In the essay "The Price of the Ticket," James Baldwin describes the critical role Williams and Delaney played in his survival and early development as a writer. Grateful acknowledgment to Jay Wright for the use of the italicized phrases from his poem "The Eye of God, the Soul's First Vision," from *Dimensions of History* (in *Transfigurations,* LSU Press © 2000 by Jay Wright).

Photograph of Beauford Delaney: Freeman family photograph, photographer unknown. Reprinted by permission of Roy Freeman.

"Terror in the Heart of Freedom": This title is borrowed from Hannah Rosen's historical study of Black freedom struggles in the post-Emancipation era, used by permission of the University of North Carolina Press. Delaney's "Untitled (Tennessee Landscape)" (1922) and "Knoxville Landscape" (1969) inspired this poem, along with accounts of the intense anti-Black violence in Knoxville during the "Red Summer" of 1919.

"Quarry (At the Isabella Stewart Gardner Museum)": Delaney frequented the Isabella Stewart Gardner Museum during his years in Boston, attending concerts there in addition to studying Gardner's eclectically curated masterpieces. The epigraphs to this poem are from Evan Charteris in *John Sargent*, Charles Scribner's Sons, 1927; Beauford Delaney's Paris journals; and Henry Louis Gates Jr., from a 1993 lecture at the Gardner Museum, quoted in *Eye of the Beholder: Masterpieces from the Isabella Stewart Gardner Museum*, the ISG Museum and Beacon Press, 2003. The phrase "a stained glass effect from the choral reality of their splendor" is from Delaney's journals. The Gardner Museum's statue of the Egyptian sky god Horus is the deity referenced in "Outdoor Interior."

"Blue Harlem": This poem's title inverts the title of a 1949 painting by Delaney. The nouns (and parenthetical parts of speech) in this poem appear in Delaney's journal entry about his traumatic first night in New York City, when he was conned out of all his belongings. David Leeming quotes this journal entry in *Amazing Grace: A Life of Beauford Delaney*, Oxford University Press, 1998.

"Sister": Beauford's sister Ogust Mae, a supplemental mother figure in the family, died in 1915, at the age of 19.

"Easy Money Is Hard to Come By": Delaney lived in an apartment on Greene Street near Washington Square for decades. The "boy" who climbs the stairs to his door in this poem is 16-year-old James Baldwin. By Baldwin's own account, he was living through crises of identity, sexuality, religious faith, and faith in the possibility of a creative life, when his friend Emile Capouya—a fellow student and literary-magazine editor at De Witt Clinton High School—who also knew Delaney, suggested that meeting the elder might benefit the younger man. "The Easy Winners" is a ragtime composition by Scott Joplin. The phrase "the luck to be Black on a Saturday night" is a quotation from Maya Angelou's poem "Weekend Glory."

"*Dark Rapture* 1941": "Dark Rapture" was the title Delaney gave to his first portrait of James Baldwin, his beloved protégé and friend. Baldwin wasn't publicly identified as the sitter for this painting until many years after its 1941 showing. "The subject of the dream is the dreamer" is a quotation from Toni Morrison's *Playing in the Dark: Whiteness and the Literary Imagination*, used by permission.

"Gratitude": In James Baldwin, Delaney found a lifelong friend and source of creative inspiration. He drew and painted Baldwin, from life and from memory, many times, and his portraits of the writer are some of his most renowned works. From Baldwin's biography, it's clear that he was aware of Delaney's initial feelings of romantic and sexual attraction to him; his feelings for the painter, while intense, seem to have always been filial. Baldwin found in Delaney the father figure he had been desperately seeking. This poem is written from the perspective of one who recognizes the pleasure and creative potential of love and desire for the lover.

"Hazing the Amiable Beauford Delaney": This is a found poem, an extended quotation from Henry Miller's essay "The Amazing and Invariable Beauford DeLaney [sic]," which brought the artist substantial attention. Delaney and Miller remained friends for life after meeting in Greenwich Village.

"Leaving Greene Street: Beauford's Psalm": This poem borrows from Psalm 30, the psalm of the House of David. Delaney, a preacher's son, would have been deeply familiar with it, as he was with many hymns and spirituals.

Drawing of Beauford Delaney: Illustrator Don Freeman, a long-standing friend of Delaney's, created this sketch, circa 1966. Housed in the Beinecke Rare Book and Manuscript Library at Yale, it is reproduced here by permission of Roy Freeman.

"In the Musée de Cluny": The Cluny Museum is France's museum of the Middle Ages. The centerpiece of its collection are the six tapestries called "The Lady and the Unicorn." Parts of the building were erected on top of Roman ruins, the Thermes de Cluny.

"Une Boîte de Nuit": In France, a *boîte de nuit* is a nightclub. Delaney's sexual desire for men was not much more socially acceptable in 1950s Paris than in mid-twentieth-century New York.

"Paris Moods: Catalogue Raisonné": This poem is composed of titles Delaney gave to his paintings.

"Canopy": The italicized line is from Phillis Wheatley's poem "On Imagination."

"How Can We Live Unmagnified among the White Colossi?": In July 1961, Delaney took a long-imagined trip to Greece. The stress of travel induced a psychotic episode during which he threw himself into the harbor at Patras. He and his belongings were rescued by local fishermen. Delaney painted the works alluded to in this poem—"Abstraction #12" and "Moving Sunlight"—in the mid-1960s, after his suicide attempt and recovery. He created some of his most impressive works in the last decade of his productive life.

"Questionnaire": This poem's entire vocabulary (with the exception of one word) is drawn from the McGill Pain Questionnaire, used worldwide to assess and categorize physical pain.

"Black Canvas": Early in the twenty-first century, art suppliers began selling black stretched canvas, which was never before available. The "Dante" mentioned in this poem is Dante Pavone, an Italian American singer with whom Delaney had an intense emotional relationship beginning in the mid-1930s. Delaney sketched and painted Pavone many times over the course of their decades-long friendship.

"Sister's Spirit Shouts": In the wake of his 1961 suicide attempt, Delaney's journals record his revived memories of his older sister, Ogust Mae, who died in 1915.

"Marian, Illuminated": In 1965, Delaney painted an extraordinary, life-size portrait of Marian Anderson, one of his favorite singers. The phrase "order composed of mass, line, plane, and color"—Delaney's definition of painterly composition—is a quotation from his journals, circa 1940. African American poet Countee Cullen befriended Delaney in Boston in the 1920s.

"Papa Bois dans la rue Vercingétorix": Toward the end of his life, Delaney lived in an apartment on this Montparnasse street, which some friends and patrons had purchased to provide him a place to live and work. Delaney's "Portrait of a Young Musician" was the catalyst for these poems. It's a very fine example of his late work, now in the collection of the Studio Museum in Harlem. The epigraph is the title of a drawing by artist William Pope.L.

"Jean Genet in the Jungle": This poem riffs off of Delaney's 1972 portrait of writer Jean Genet.

"Coming to Saint Paul": As his psychiatric condition worsened in the early 1970s, Delaney wrote many letters he never sent. This poem quotes extensively from one such letter to James Baldwin, in which Delaney was inviting himself to stay at the writer's house in Saint-Paul-de-Vence, where he was always a welcome guest. In the original letter, now archived in the Schomburg Center for Research in Black Culture, Delaney refers to the imagined presence of the saint in the town named for him. I've also quoted and paraphrased lines from Saint Paul's first letter to the Corinthians, merging the biblical text with Delaney's voice. 1 Corinthians contains some of Delaney's favorite New Testament passages.

"Writing You from a Plague Year": I drafted a significant portion of this collection during the global coronavirus pandemic of 2020–21. The epigraph is from *"loco moveri"* from *Asked What Has Changed,* 20. © 2021 by Ed Roberson. Published by Wesleyan University Press. Used by permission.

"My Memory Stammers: But My Soul Is a Witness": Joseph Delaney (1904–1991), Beauford's younger brother, was a celebrated painter in his own right. He moved to New York City in 1930. Beauford's biographer attests to their mutual love and pride in one another's work, as evidenced by their warm correspondence and the tales each told about the other. However, their relationship was also marked by Joseph's disapproval of Beauford's queerness and some aspects of his lifestyle. The title of this poem, punctuation included, is a quotation from James Baldwin's *The Evidence of Things Not Seen,* Henry Holt and Company, 1985.

"Final Prayer: To Beauford D. (1976)": "Destinations are one's true originations" is a quotation from Robert Stepto's introduction to Jay Wright's *Selected Poems,* Princeton University Press, 1987, used by permission of the author. This poem is informed by photos of Delaney from 1976, when he was being cared for in St. Anne's Psychiatric Hospital in Paris.

"a rite": *Minkisi* (the plural of *nkisi*) are spiritually invested objects in the Kongo cultural world and in parts of the African Diaspora. They are functional spiritual objects—"things that do things."

Printed in the United States
by Baker & Taylor Publisher Services